Reuse and RECYCLE

by Michèle Dufresne

WE
RECYCLE

Pioneer Valley Educational Press, Inc.

TABLE OF CONTENTS

A WORLD OF GARBAGE

Did you know that there is more
and more garbage in the world
with each passing day?
The average American produces
about 4.4 pounds of garbage a day,
totaling 30.8 pounds per week
and 1,606 pounds a year.

Our trash cans are full.
Our streets and roadsides are littered.
Our oceans and rivers are **polluted** with trash.

Long ago, people did not create much garbage. They repaired and reused most of what they had.

Today, machines can make things quickly and cheaply. People often choose to buy something new rather than repair something old.

In recent years, people began producing **disposable** items. People now buy things like disposable pens, disposable razors, and disposable diapers. This has created even more garbage.

e-WASTE

There is a new kind of trash
called electronic waste, or e-waste,
which is taking up space in our landfills.
E-waste comes from old electronic items
that have been thrown away. Some kinds
of electronic equipment are thrown away
when they break or wear out.

E-waste includes big items
like washing machines and small items
like cell phones. Many electronic products
are thrown away even though they still work
because people want a new model
with new features.

Some electronic equipment
is hard to recycle because it is made
from many different materials
that cannot be reused unless the equipment
is taken apart. Often **toxic** substances
are found in e-waste. This is a big problem
for our landfills.

LANDFILLS

In the United States, most of our trash is hauled to a landfill by garbage trucks. At the landfill, a compactor crushes the piles of trash. Bulldozers cover up the piles with dirt to prevent odors and to keep rats and flies away.

Landfills are filling up fast. It is becoming harder and harder to find places for new landfills because people do not want to live near one.

Some countries do not have
enough landfills for all their trash,
and other countries do not have any landfills.

Some countries do not have garbage trucks
to pick up their trash. Because of this,
people sometimes dump their trash
into streets, rivers, and oceans.

POLLUTION

Garbage creates pollution.
As the trash in a landfill breaks down,
it releases toxic gases.

Many scientists believe
that some of these gases
are raising the earth's temperature
by trapping the sun's energy.
This is just part of a bigger problem
that scientists call global warming.

When trash is dumped into the ocean, the ocean water can break down some, but not all, of the waste. Sometimes fish and other sea animals swallow the toxic waste. If we eat these fish and sea animals, the toxins can end up in our bodies and make us sick.

There is a huge amount of plastic waste in the ocean. Plastic is a problem for marine life. Some marine animals eat pieces of plastic and become sick. They can also become tangled in a piece of plastic waste, such as a plastic bag.

Even chewing gum can cause pollution!
Gum is very difficult to clean up because
it is sticky and hard to remove from sidewalks
and streets. It does not break down, so it stays
in the **environment** for a long time.

REDUCE AND REUSE

There are many ways to reduce the amount of garbage we throw away each day.

The first thing you can do is think before you buy something new. Do you really need that item?

When you are shopping, try to choose products that have little or no packaging. Take a reusable shopping bag with you instead of using paper or plastic bags from the store.

Try to use products that you can use again and again. For example, use a refillable water bottle instead of buying plastic bottles of water.

RECYCLE TRASH

We can reduce the amount of trash in landfills by recycling some of our garbage.

Paper, glass, aluminum cans, plastic, and many other objects can be recycled into new things.

WE
RECYCLE

Composting is another way to recycle. Instead of throwing away leftover fruits and vegetables, you can compost them.

To make compost, place leftover fruits and vegetables in a hole in the ground or in a special container and allow it to **decompose**. Compost can be used as fertilizer to help grow new plants and vegetables.

If more people reuse and recycle,
there will be less garbage,
and our planet will be a cleaner,
healthier place to live.

GLOSSARY

decompose: to rot

disposable: designed to be thrown away after use

environment: the circumstances, objects, or conditions by which one is surrounded

polluted: made unclean or contaminated

toxic: extremely harsh, malicious, or harmful

INDEX